Journey through ATLANTA
WITH JIYAH

JIYAH FENNELL

FENNELL ADVENTURES

Journey through Atlanta with Jiyah
Copyright © 2018 by Jiyah Fennell

All rights reserved. No part of this book may be reproduced or transmitted in any form or by any means without written permission from the author.

ISBN 978-1-7324796-5-4

Printed in the United States of America

Publishing info: Fennell Adventures LLC
info@fennelladventures.com
678-895-7468

How to read this book:

This is **NOT** your ordinary, read each page from start to finish book!
You will decide which order your Atlanta adventure will go.
All you have to do is choose between the pages in the color **RED.**
This way you can read this same book several times in a variety of ways.
Enjoy ! 🙂

Hey everybody, my name is Jiyah and I live in Atlanta, Georgia. I'll be your amazing tour guide today as I show you the city and its surrounding areas. I promise you'll have fun. C'mon! I'll show you!

God is a key component in my life. We have to start the day off by giving him the praise and the glory that he deserves. "Dear God, direct and order our steps as we explore these streets of Atlanta. In Jesus' name we pray, Amen".

The city of Atlanta is full of food, fun, films, and famous people. People from all over want to come and see the fancy cars and homes. Many entrepreneurs live here, and they make their dreams come true. You can make your dreams come true, too! They say this city never sleeps! You can find something to do any day of the week.

This is an awesome adventure book where YOU decide how the story goes, so choose wisely. Once we get going, tell me exactly where you would like to go first.

The first place we'll be going is the famous Centennial Park. I'm sure you know it already, but I'll show you anyway. Centennial Olympic Park is downtown in the heart of Atlanta.

This is sad, but in 1996 many people died in a bombing. The park has a memorial in remembrance of those people. Please take a moment of silence in their honor. (Pause) A lot of events occur here such as Wind down Wednesday during the summer and other concerts. I really like the water fountain that dances to music. Check it out!

If you would like to grab a snack from Six Flags, let's go to page 12.

If you would like to have some fun at Main Event, let's go to page 18.

Now we are at the World's largest Aquarium, the Georgia Aquarium and there's so much to do here. We can sit down to watch the dolphin show and let the water splash on us. Another option is to touch the sting rays. We could also grab some 4D glasses and head to the theatre to watch a show. I say we step onto the escalator and ride through the tunnel to see all of the amazing creatures surrounding us. Wow! That shark is pretty cool!

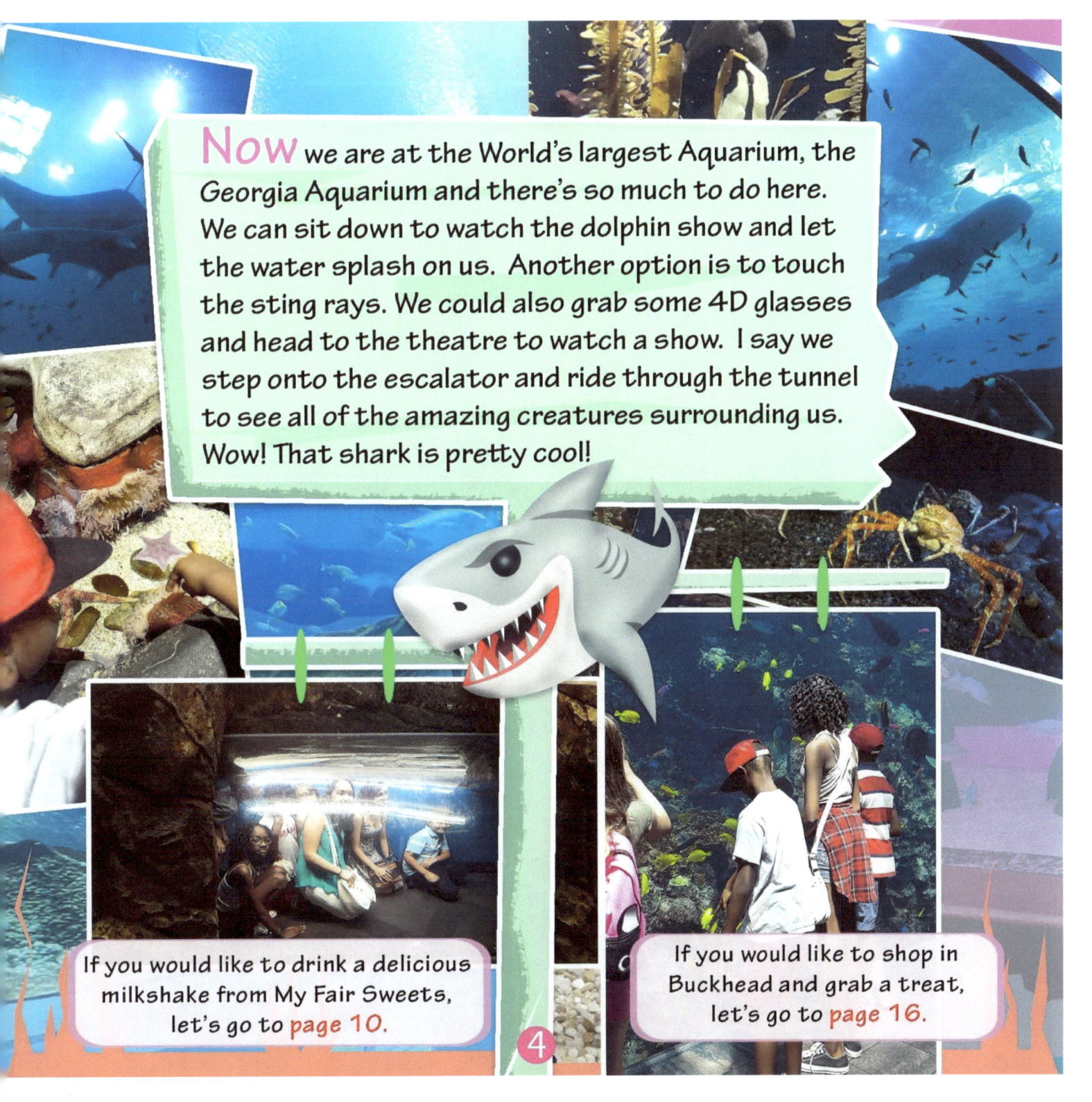

If you would like to drink a delicious milkshake from My Fair Sweets, let's go to page 10.

If you would like to shop in Buckhead and grab a treat, let's go to page 16.

Can you name a drink that brings you happiness? Of course you said Coke! You cannot come to Atlanta and not stop by the World of Coca-Cola. It is right next to the aquarium, so let's walk over. As you watch the happy video, you are quickly reminded of all of the great memories people have experienced with Coke. This video really makes me happy! Being able to taste all of the Coke flavors throughout the world makes me happy, too! I like Delaware Punch. Which flavor is your favorite? How about we do a cheer with the free classic sample bottle that they give to us? Cheers to my friend!

If you would like to grab a burger from The Varsity, let's go to page 8.

If you would like to grab some BBQ food from Jim N' Nick's, let's go to page 17.

If you are anything like my lil' brother, Merl, you love basketball. In the ATL, the Atlanta Hawks play at Phillips Arena. This place is used for basketball games and concerts.

Shhh, listen closely, do you hear that? It's my favorite singer, Ariana Grande. We are actually sitting in the arena right now as she graces the stage. Join my friend, Jayla, and me. There are thousands of fans in the building, but we have some great seats! I am her #1 fan and would love to meet her someday. Sing along with me, "Ain't got no tears left to cryyyyyyyy." Who would you like to see here at the Phillips Arena?

If you would like to see creatures at the Georgia Aquarium, let's go to page 4.

If you would like to shop at Lenox Mall, let's go to page 13.

Do you like watching CNN? Then you will really like where we are now. We are at the CNN Center.

This is their headquarters, and its right here in Atlanta. The main news rooms and studios are inside of this building. They even have an activity where you can pretend to be a news anchor. Isn't that cool?

Your only choice is to end this adventure, so sadly we will go to page 20 ☹

Are you hungry? Well, that's good because we're now at The Varsity. There are so many delicious options on the menu! Chili burgers, peach pies, onion rings, chicken sandwiches, and more. The lines inside are always long, but they do move fast. Let's fill our stomachs with some of this delightful food. What do you think? It tastes good, RIGHT?

If you would like to grab a baseball from SunTrust Park Stadium, let's go to page 15.

If you would like to end this adventure, let's go to page 20.

Are you a huge football fan? Then you may remember 2017 when the Atlanta Falcons went to the Super Bowl. It was a big deal in the "A"! I was even called to utilize my professional face painting skills at a celebrity's home. That was a memorable event for me.

Now that the Mercedes-Benz Stadium has been built, the next Super Bowl will be hosted here. Look around at this place, isn't it fabulous?

If you would like to check out the CNN Center, let's go to page 7.

If you would like to see a great view from Stone Mountain, let's go to page 14.

"**Milkshakes,** milkshakes, milkshakes", or should I say it again, "milkshakes"! OMG! is all I can say about these famous over the top milkshakes! My Fair Sweets is a restaurant & bakery located in downtown Atlanta.

Look at these monstrous shakes! Cheat Day is for that one day you can cheat with your calories. It has not one, not two, but three vanilla donuts covered with sprinkles! We can lick the side of the cup because it is covered with sprinkles. This vanilla shake is even topped with whipped cream. Are you willing to share, or would you like your own?

If you would like to grab a burger from The Varsity, let's go to page 8.

If you would like to end this adventure, let's go to page 20.

I think unity is very important. I also think following your dreams is important, too! Well, it is important that we stop by the historical site of one of the most famous men that changed history. That's right! Martin Luther King Jr. believed in unity and having a dream as well. This is the house where he grew up. Inside of the building, you can learn all about the change he made and see garments that he wore. On the outside of the building, you can see the sites where he and his wife, Coretta Scott King, are buried in the water. Let's pay our respects to such a great family. Please close your eyes and bow your heads. Thank you MLK for the sacrifices that you made.

If you would like to check out the CNN Center, let's go to page 7.

If you would like to grab a baseball from SunTrust Park Stadium, let's go to page 15.

As a teenager, of course I love to shop. Let's head to the infamous Lenox Mall. Look around at all of these stores. This mall is always crowded with people. A lot of famous people shop here. We may bump into one of them while we are here. Who would you like to bump into?

If you would like to see the new Mercedes Benz Stadium, let's go to page 9.

If you would like to grab a baseball from SunTrust Park Stadium, let's go to page 15.

Let's step outside of the city of Atlanta for a second. We are headed to Stone Mountain Park. They have a ton of activities to explore. We can climb the rock wall, sky ride, miniature golf, duck boat, hike, or enjoy a film at the 4D theatre just to name a few. The mountain is HUGE, and you can walk or sky ride to the top. How do you prefer to see this scenic view?

If you would like to grab a burger from The Varsity, let's go to page 8.

If you would like to end this adventure, let's go to page 20.

"Take me out to the ball game, take me out with the crowd." We are singing loudly because we are now at SunTrust Park. This is where Atlanta's official baseball team, the Atlanta Braves, plays. Look around at this brand-new stadium. Let's grab a seat and a baseball mitt because we might just catch a ball.

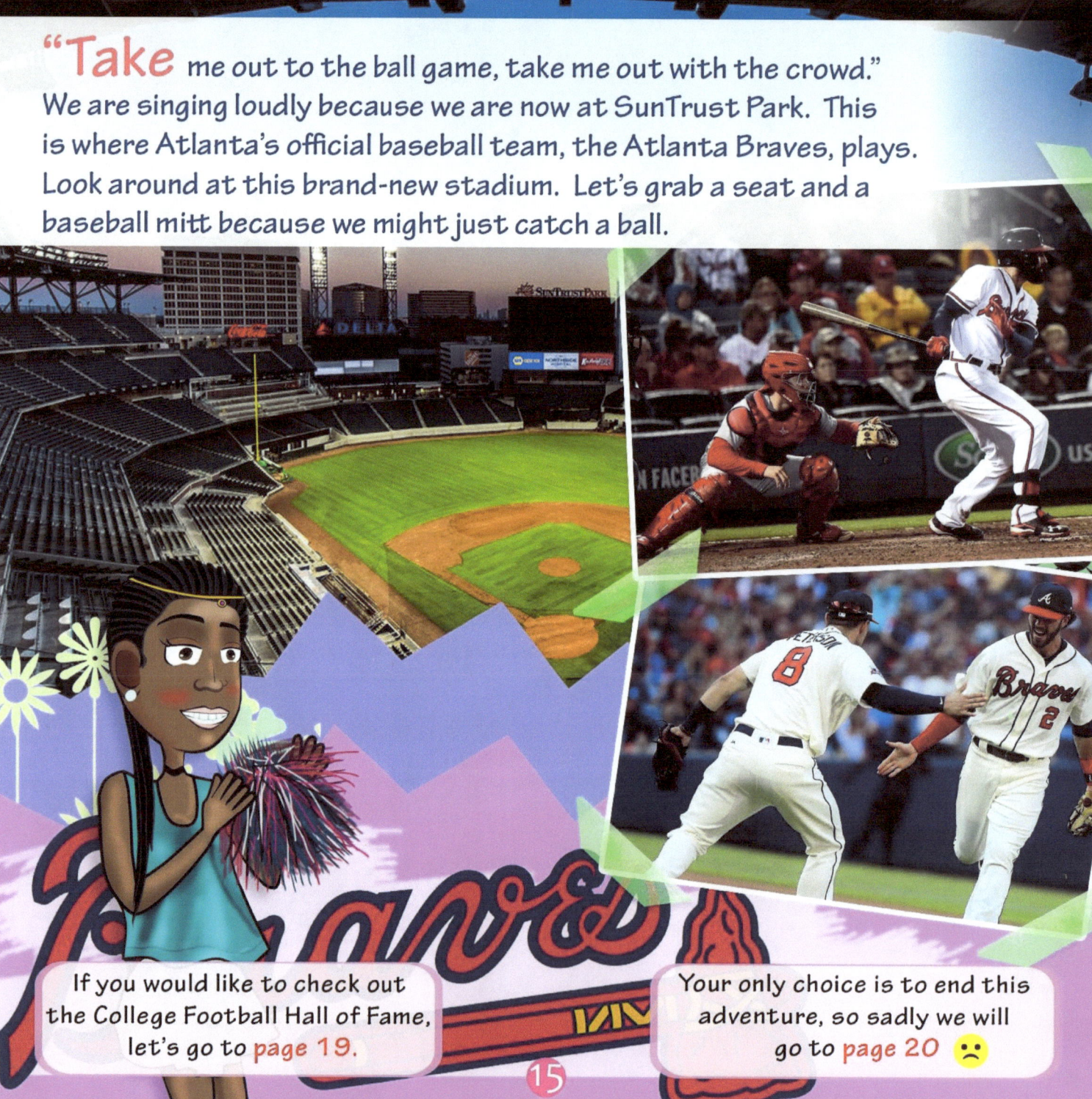

If you would like to check out the College Football Hall of Fame, let's go to page 19.

Your only choice is to end this adventure, so sadly we will go to page 20 ☹

Don't you love to shop? We are headed to some luxury stores in Buckhead Atlanta. We can shop, grab a bite to eat, or just browse the art. We have got to grab a delicious cupcake from my mom's favorite spot here, Georgetown Cupcakes! It's cupcake heaven. What's your favorite cupcake?

If you would like to see a great view from Stone Mountain, let's go to page 14.

If you would like to end this adventure, let's go to page 20.

Are you in the mood for some barbeque? Well, let' pull up a chair at Jim 'N Nick's Bar-B-Q. OMG! Look at all of the choices! There are cheese biscuits, burgers, salads, mac n cheese, and more. My personal favorite are the chicken drummies with fresh fruit. How about we grab a seat and dig in. Let me know what you want from the menu.

If you would like to check out the CNN Center, let's go to page 7.

If you would like to shop at Lenox Mall, let's go to page 13.

Is your middle name fun? If not, it is now. That's because we are having a ton of fun at Main Event. There are arcade games, bowling, great food, laser tag, and more. I say we hit the gravity ropes. Be careful to hold on and don't look down!

If you would like to quench your thirst at the World of Coke, let's go to page 5.

If you would like to see where MLK grew up, let's go to page 11.

I'm only 14 years old, so I have never been to a college football game yet. It won't be long until I get to experience the excitement that comes along with Alabama Crimson Tide vs Georgia Bulldogs. Until then let's check out the College Football Hall of Fame.

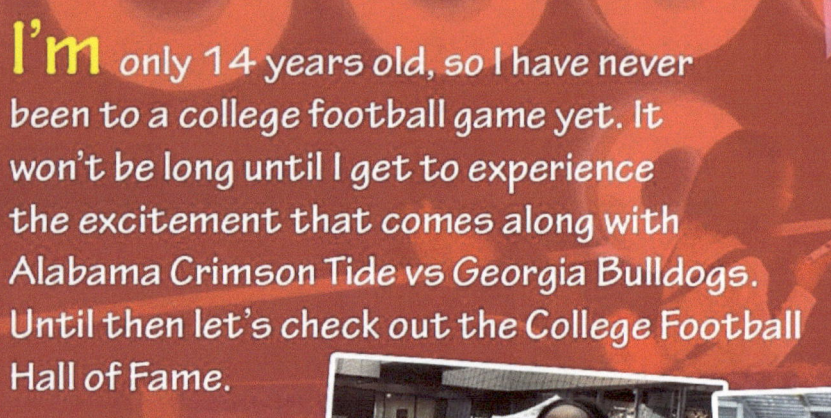

This place is football fan heaven. You see that football field. We can go over and actually kick a field goal. There are so many other interactive fun things to do like pretend to be a football anchor, sing football karaoke, virtual games, and more. Grab your virtual eyewear so we can head to a college football game!

Your only choice is to end this adventure, so sadly we will go to page 20 😞

Ok! We have come to the end of the adventure. Let us talk. What do you think of the city Atlanta? I hope you get as excited about the ATL like I do! We just had a great time together, but we were not alone. God was with us the entire time just as he is in real life. All you have to do is ask him for the desires of your heart, and they will be granted to you. May God bless you.

Jiyah-
A daughter just like yours!

Start another Atlanta Adventure from the beginning!

www.ingramcontent.com/pod-product-compliance
Lightning Source LLC
LaVergne TN
LVHW071031070426
835507LV00002B/105